The Only Girl in the Room

Real Life Tales of
One Woman's Climb Up the Corporate Ladder

By Nancy L. Bullock

ISBN: 1519399561
ISBN-13: 978-1519399564

DEDICATION

To the man who planted me with his love and helped me to grow me into a
real live writer and WOMAN who could hear her own voice:

Andrew Dale Bullock
Aka MY Andy
Yup
Love You

CONTENTS

Acknowledgments   i

Prologue   1

Foundation   3

1   The Glamour of it All!   5

2   The Game   9

3   "My Thought"   11

4   On Becoming a Man   15

5   A Word or Two About the "F" Bomb   19

6   The Crying Game   21

7   Shh… Don't Tell Anyone I'm a Mother   24

8   The Problem is <u>Not</u> Men   29

9   The Solution is <u>Not</u> Women   33

10   TOO   36

11   I am a Human Firewall   38

12   That Was Then, This Is Now   41

13   My Mother   45

14   My Guilty Secret   48

15   Now What?   52

ACKNOWLEDGMENTS

Cast of Characters

There are many people in my life who made it possible for me to "get into the room." I am grateful to them, because I really wanted to get into that room, even though being there was a mixed bag of blessings. And while this book is all about concepts and ideas and not naming the names of those who were both really good and bad in my journey, I need to acknowledge the following people in my life who made the journey *even possible*.

Herb Laney
The Ideal Mentor (still)

Penny Barnas Powell
The Protégé, Chicago Best Friend

Alicia Rizzo Middleton
The Cheerleader, Michigan Best Friend

Andy Wandell
The Best Business "Brother", Lifelong Supporting Fan

Christopher G. Hamlin
The Supportive First Husband

Julia E. Harrington and Andrew R. Hamlin
The World's Best Kids Ever

Aaron Leopold
The Amazing Cover Artist and Oldest Hamlin Nephew

Gloria Jane Bruner Keyser
The Crazy but Wonderful Mother, RIP

.

PROLOGUE

So, who in the world **AM I** and why should you read this book?

I am a very ambitious, competitive small town girl who got a job in the business world (not her first choice) and started her corporate business career in 1981. Maybe like you, maybe like your wife or your sister or your girlfriend. (If your girlfriend started her career in 1981, you should marry her, buddy, the clock is ticking.)

To refresh your memory, 1981 was the year that Ronald Reagan was elected President to his first term, the annual inflation rate was at 10.35%, interest rates were at 15.75%, Sandra Day O'Connor was nominated to become the FIRST female Supreme Court Justice, IBM launched the first PC, the MTV cable channel was born and Princess Diana married Prince Charles in a spectacular wedding watched around the world. Wow. 1981 was definitely a while ago. Which makes me a girl (Ha!!) decidedly not starting out my career, but a girl looking back at what went right and what went wrong over the past 34 years. Yikes!!

I am not a sociologist or a business psychologist. I am not a business coach. I don't even have a MBA! I don't know anymore if I am even a feminist. I don't know what that means in this day and age. I want women to have options. I want women to be taken as seriously as they want to be taken. I also want women to be paid what they should be paid for the contributions that they make in an organization. That would be, the SAME AS MEN.

I do know that I am a woman who thinks that being a woman is GREAT, who has a GREAT daughter and who thinks other women are GREAT as well.

The reflections I share in this book are a compilation of the often comical observations, experiences and tensions I personally experienced in

1

MY OWN up and down business career - specifically around the myriad of ideas I had imprinted from my mother's unrealized ambitions, the ideas I had been bathed in from the 60's and 70's mass media, ideas I had picked up from the culture-at-large and ideas I formulated based on my own personal ambitions about what *"a woman's business career should and would look like starting out in 1981."*

1981 was the beginning of an interesting period of time in the United States corporate business sector and country at large. Women heard that major changes were being proposed in the work world. The *US Census Bureau Data* shows that women in the work force grew from 14.8 million in 1967 to 22 million in 1981. Women in manager positions climbed from just under 15% in 1960 to 25% in 1981. Corporations were in the beginning stages of change. The idea that women needed to be taken seriously as managers and directors and senior managers was gaining a certain amount of momentum and mainstream media coverage. It seemed as if it was going to be possible to pass the Equal Rights Amendment (ERA) into the Constitution. Change was in the air, accompanied by a strong feeling of hope and vision from my vantage point.

I think my story is one that many of you have experienced in some way or another. I say that from hearing my female friends, female and male colleagues and female coworkers tell me their own personal stories. And I think that is why I feel it is important to tell this story. I have spoken with so many women over the past few years who started out their business journey at the same time as mine, many even 10 years after mine and they have ended up "hitting the wall" or that very clear "glass ceiling", the full cliché of which you can't appreciate until you give yourself a concussion beating your head against it. Ouch!! These women are disillusioned. These women are really tired. They feel shame. They feel blame. These women feel like they have failed. Failed at what?

I do not believe that we can cultivate yet another generation of businesswomen who feel marginalized and discouraged about their jobs, their chances for success and equal pay and their chances for making a difference in the corporate world. Yes, this is very hard stuff, complicated and without easy or quick answers. But let's not give up yet. I think our society can be smart about this, can be smart about making changes, listening and becoming better about blending the workforce in all ways – male, female, Hispanic, African-American, Asian, straight, gay – we all need to work together. We need the bench strength. An "all white male bench" is not enough to compete globally in the marketplace anymore. It's just not.

Just look around you.

THE FOUNDATION

Like many women who graduated from college in 1981, (*Michigan State University*, a good solid mid-western "in-state" school for me, nothing fancy) I had been given dreams and goals and ambitions based on culture, family dynamics, education levels, my parent's aspirations and finally, my own aspirations as well. Right, wrong or indifferent, they influenced what I thought my life would be like in the business world.

I started out my journey in 1959 at *Madison General Hospital* in Madison, WI and my parents named me Nancy Louise Keyser. My father was finishing up a graduate degree in agricultural science at the University of Wisconsin and my mom was an elementary schoolteacher and the "PhD dissertation typist and editor" for my dad. My mom was 30 and my dad was 32. I was my parent's first child after 10 years of marriage, which was not common for that time. They were married in 1949.

We moved to Kalamazoo, MI when I was 6 years old in 1965. (Yes, I am a "gal" from Kalamazoo, for all of you who are over 95, you'll get the reference!) My dad had a good job at *The Upjohn Company* (a pharmaceuticals and research company) because of his PhD training and schooling, but was not a corporate star by any means. My parents were both extremely smart, ambitious and hardworking, but they were not wealthy nor privileged nor unique. They were from modest upbringings in the heartland of Nebraska, along the Platte River, Kearney and Shelton respectively.

My mother was driven and smart, but not assertive or rebellious. My mother should have gone into the business and corporate world. But since she didn't (at that time, if your husband had a good job, "the wife" just didn't work because it would look like your husband couldn't support you), and consequently, I think she pushed both my father and me into that direction. And we were both fairly unhappy with those decisions. Okay, often miserable. But hey, we could have pushed back and we didn't. Where

3

was our backbone? I would say that my mother cast a large shadow of unrealized desire, and we fell under the cloud of her own longing and working ambitions.

However, my mother's underlying aspirations for me (herself) played nicely into the changing female/work cultural landscape in the 1970's that helped create expectations about what my future could be. For what my future SHOULD be.

Our family was financially comfortable and had many material things, but were absolutely not "well-off", not even upper-middle class in income when I think back. We stuck to budgets, did not belong to the community country clubs like some of my friends, did not travel internationally like some of my friends. Most of our summer vacations growing up were long, cramped, 14-hour car rides back to Nebraska to see my parent's extended families. My mother made it clear to me that we did not have "family money" to fall back on either. It was up to her and my father to provide and invest for me and my younger brother, Paul.

So, I would say that growing up in Kalamazoo, Michigan in the 1960's and 70's, my family was solidly "middle-class regular". I studied very hard all through my school career, pushed myself and wanted to make my parents proud of me – but there were so many other people who graduated in the Loy Norrix High School Class of 1977 with more impressive pedigrees than mine. I was not voted the most likely to succeed. I was not a valedictorian, although I did graduate with honors, but not with high honors or a National Merit Scholarship. I don't know if anyone would have predicted that I would end up in the top "1%" of corporate executive women in terms of job status and salary. In re-reading my high school yearbook comments from friends, I apparently looked very driven, though I do not remember that trait so much in high school as in college.

I had big plans and desires for my future, but I would say they were vaguely cast to start. I had not gone to an Ivy League school; my academic pedigree in college was slightly more impressive than high school, finishing up with Phi Beta Kappa honors. But my focus for most of my college career was on writing and I capped off my English studies by also being Editor-in-Chief of the MSU yearbook during my senior year.

I "started out" wanting to be a writer, whatever that means, but ended up taking a job at Procter and Gamble because it was sure thing, a solid company and quite honestly, I was impressed by how impressed everyone was that I got a offered a job there. Perhaps not the most auspicious start to a budding career. But anyway, that's my story and I am sticking to it. So…here we go!!

1

THE GLAMOUR OF IT ALL!

The CEO hates me. And in all honesty, I didn't really understand how strong his feelings were until THIS conference call. Yes, I am not totally unaware of his dislike for me, I can personally tell that he doesn't like my answers to his questions much of the time, he usually wants me to go back and produce a different answer (yet, why would the same process generate new data?) but I have just enough self-esteem not to immediately go to "the CEO must hate me". And I was also possibly in protective denial. I have been with this company for 4 years and my division has been profitable and paid out bonuses. I am a "proven" executive, not anyone new, and my views should not be surprising, nor controversial at this stage in my relationship with the company. Four years in.

HE is the CEO, strictly by birthright, not by talent or skill or ambition. His brother started the company and had the "really big idea" and then HE came into the organization and is just along for the ride as far as I can tell. However, this CEO is just smart enough to feel very insecure about this family/business scenario, so he has cultivated the very attractive management style of "business bully". It also appears that HE revels in making female employees feel especially small and stupid by asking them an ungodly amount of small and stupid questions that he NEVER asks the men.

In one typical meeting, I watch this CEO demean one of the smartest women in the company over the "appearance" of her data. It was not formatted according to what he would like to see. But it WAS great data. And it was the right data. And if you were smart enough, you would have noticed that it was the right data you were looking for and you wouldn't have spent **30 minutes** talking about her formatting. He could not get past the formatting issue. It was…comical in retrospect, but truly surreal during the meeting.

And then, I have seen some of the men on this team share their anecdotal views without ANY supporting data (when that was undeniably called for), just literally share their top-of-mind opinions and views, obviously un-showered, un-groomed, their hair sticking out of the side of their heads, barely presentable and overtly hung over from a previous night of revelry, and all is well with the world! The CEO is FINE with "THAT GUY'S" opinion not supported by data, let alone data formatted in any way to his special specifications. Needless to say, this is discussed in detail by my fellow women colleagues behind closed doors. The differences in expectations are not subtle. They are blatant. These differences are something my fellow women colleagues and I are not happy about. But we try to manage.... we try to manage HIM... and HIS insecurities, HIS craziness and HIS general inability to run the company effectively. Yup.

"We", are a very small group of female executives, and try our best to back each other up in these ridiculously long, tense meetings, designed to give the CEO something solid to do with his day. As I wonder about the true definition of fun, I am fairly certain it is not these meetings. And I am also certain that these women are totally wonderful, competent and tough. These women would make your profit number AND take a bullet for you if you were in our circle. These are GREAT women.

So, I was beginning a regular Thursday morning at 9:00 AM in my suburban Chicago office. I am getting ready to go on the bi-weekly update call with the New York headquarters' office. I thought it was going to be just another conference call presentation among many conference call presentations that I have done at this company over the past FOUR years. Conference calls are always awkward and challenging because I need to be very convincing, persuasive and authoritative sounding over the phone without being able to use the power of my actual physical presence in the room, which is always an advantage.

When I woke up this specific morning, brushed my teeth, put on my make-up and drank my coffee, I had no idea that TODAY would totally create for me a very bizarre reputation in the company, test every single executive coaching "role play" I have ever been through in my career, and show me that I am far stronger than I ever thought. How was I to know that today would establish the foundation and set the stage for my last day at this company, would seal the deal for me being famous and infamous, gaining me both respect and pity at the same time? Who really knows this stuff when they wake up on a regular Thursday morning and drive into work?

So, what really happened during that 90-minute "legendary" conference call? I wish I could remember all of the details of the truly ridiculous exchange that landed me in the handicap stall in the women's bathroom doing Lamaze breathing, while THREE senior male executives in our

Chicago office labored in our executive conference room about how to "handle the problem of me". This was AFTER the CEO called the Division President to say whatever he said about my glaring and unforgivable deficiencies. Huge wooden conference doors were flying shut. "Important" executive men were huddled together having heated conversations. This was obviously very serious. This was a BIG problem. Correction, I WAS THE BIG PROBLEM. My stomach hurt, my head hurt, I felt dizzy and disoriented. I often love being the center of attention, but not for being "bad". And I knew I had been "bad." Bad Nancy.

This conference call brought to light the huge problem of "me" following and executing the marketing strategy of my immediate boss, who was the division CEO and who loved to blatantly defy the corporate CEO, brother of the founder. I found myself caught very firmly in the middle of a classic power struggle between my direct boss and the CEO of the entire family owned company. Oops. While it was completely ridiculous, MY big mistake was overtly supporting my immediate boss, which made the CEO absolutely livid. I am assuming he was feeling totally threatened because he actually had very little control over my division's business, so the process of having that fact "thrown" in his face during a meeting made him VERY mad. Oh yeah, really, really mad!! Whew!

OK, so I probably need more coaching on how to appropriately verbally respond and maneuver so that "the CEO" never feels threatened or challenged, but some days stuff just pops out of your mouth and then you are screwed. Totally. Exhausting.

HE came very close to hanging up the phone on me while a dozen other executives were also in the room in New York. How did I know this was as bad as I felt it was? I actually got SYMPATHY calls afterwards from other colleagues on the conference call that were shocked, embarrassed and REALLY relieved it wasn't them. And can I tell you, those phone calls of support were weird. "Oh, yes, you really made him mad this time, Nancy, wow, wasn't that really funny when he was trying to shame and blame you and throw you against the wall? Ha, ha. I'm super glad it wasn't me. OMG, that was my first meeting with him, I couldn't believe what was happening and how calmly you handled everything". I was hugely embarrassed and very mad but also felt, in a weird sort of way, like I held my own ground in the "CEO smack down" as one executive coined it. UGH. It was absolutely one of the worst experiences of my business career. UGH. Sometimes, UGH is the only appropriate word. UGH.

The immediate solution created from all of the slamming of doors and meetings of the serious-faced male executives conferring over "the problem of me" was to have one of three senior male executives ALWAYS be on the phone with me whenever I talked to the CEO. This was the solution created behind all of those closed doors on that Thursday afternoon. One of the three male executives came into my office, solemnly closed the door and said that either "he, or the President of my brand or the President of my division would be on the phone with me for every one of these calls going forward". Also, I needed to forward to all of them the Power Point presentation I was going to share the day before the conference call.

Deep breath. Really? Wow. Wow. Wow. I need to have someone on the phone with me when I talk to the CEO. As......protection? As......backup? As.........a babysitter? Because...I am dangerous? Because I am a wild card and need to be controlled? Maybe because the CEO is totally insecure and incompetent? (Just sharing my real internal thoughts!!)

I must admit it is hard to be completely honest with myself even to this day about how truly horrible I felt when presented with "the solution". I was hurt. I did keep smiling. I did say, "yes, of course I agree!" – to the totally absurd conclusion to the problem of me and then experienced yet another piece of my business self-esteem biting the dust. I felt shame. I felt degraded. I felt like I was STILL the problem. I felt simply horrible. I am ashamed to admit that I am still trying not to feel horrible. I have also been told therapy can take awhile...

Yes, I did go back to work the next day. And believe it or not, I scored big points for that too. I was smiling. For the record, I was a single mom and I had a daughter to get through college. I had a son in high school. Even though I had not needed a babysitter for MYSELF for a very long time, I apparently was in dire need of this now at my place of employment. I was 53. I was a Vice President. Yup. "Babysitter needed for Nancy NOW. Watch out, she might poke a knife in an electrical socket or tumble down the stairs and break something." I wonder, how much do you get paid for babysitting ME?

Perhaps there is equality in the workplace somewhere. Sounds good. Seems good. I want it. I'm all for it! But I am still waiting for all of that equality to come showering down upon me while I continue to "play this business game".

Business Wisdom Nugget #1: The women's bathroom handicap stall is a very good place to cry and pray as men debate the "problem of you" and to deep breathe when you are feeling overwhelmed. But just for the record, I DID NOT CRY that day. I decided HE wasn't worth it. YAY for me!!!

2

THE GAME

So what exactly, is "the game"? While I certainly get paid more money than a female executive from some time long ago when then were NO female executives, it still is not as much as a male executive colleague. AND now, I get the additional honor to be in charge of all of the business heavy lifting – yearly, monthly and weekly budgeting, meeting profit and loss goals, recruiting, training and leading a full staff, making the bonus targets so that over 100 people in the building will receive a yearly bonus, yet, I still feel like I can never really win. Because, even in this day and age, I am "the girl". When things are going well, there is a wall of men standing in the "credit line" and I have a hard time being noticed even though I am 5' 10" and actually enormously persuasive, appropriately assertive and a strong leader. But, interestingly enough, when things are going poorly, I am so visible; you can see me from North Dakota. Several men at my company actually uttered the words, "Nancy, you need to sit in the middle of the table so that you can be the eye candy", OR, "you are the eye candy." Did I train to be the "eye candy?" REALLY? But darn it if I wasn't secretly flattered. Bad Nancy.

I am the only girl in the meeting, the only girl at the important dinner, the only girl at the boardroom table, the only girl on the phone, the only girl in the room. And while the broadcast news and a few Silicon Valley female superstars say otherwise, being the only girl in the room. ...SUCKS. And is not unusual at all. I know there are others of you out there – YOU are the only girl in the room at your company at the appropriate level to be seen with the MEN in charge. And just like me…. you feel, can I say it?, "honored" to be asked. I know. I get it. Blah. Don't apologize. At least you are in the room.

I have an image of a few male executives looking at each other in a total panic, saying, "OMG, this - fill in the blank: event, meeting, conference or dinner - is all men, let's get Nancy"…. and then thinking internally, 'she can be our female representative for this experience'. "Someone call her and ask her."

Oh, and by the way, I am NOT a girl. I am in my 50's. I am absolutely a woman. And even an executive. Maybe even elderly!! And I have made my companies and the senior executives in them a lot of money. It's often hard to stomach that I am not on the "A" list. I am on the "female token representative" list. But I am asked to go, often at the last minute, and I go willingly. Otherwise, how can I be the only girl in the room?

Perhaps this sounds whiny. A word really only used for women. Have you ever heard anyone call a man "whiny" when he is voicing his direct opinion or displeasure? "Yea, that Joe was whining all afternoon about how he didn't have enough staff to meet our business objectives this year. Whiny, Whiny, Whiny. Joe needs to buck up". I have never heard that. Just saying…

For a whole variety of reasons, I keep smiling and working and doing what I need to do to get the job done. Yet I am not on the "A" team." It appears that I am the fill-in and model of sexual diversity and balance. One white woman = Balance AND Diversity. Where did I go wrong? Did I? Oh no, there she goes being "whiny" again!

Business Wisdom Nugget #2: Always accept the invitation to be the only girl, but don't get too excited about it. It doesn't necessarily mean that are that you are valued – you are filling a spot that needs to be filled. However, since you ARE there, make the most of it. Work it!

3

"MY THOUGHT"

When I graduated from Michigan State University in 1981, I was living and grooving on the soundtrack to Gloria Gaynor's, *"I Will Survive"*, *"Hit Me With Your Best Shot"* by Pat Benatar, and *"I Am Woman"* by Helen Reddy. The Equal Rights Amendment was in the process of being ratified and the reading on my night stand included *The Women's Room* by Marilyn French, *Ms. Magazine*, and *A Room of One's Own*, by Virginia Woolf.

One of the ever-present commercials splattered all over network TV in 1980 was for a women's perfume that had a very seductive jingle that included *" I can bring home the bacon... fry it up in a pan... and never let you forget you're a man.* The 8-hour perfume, for the 24 hour woman." The "she" in this commercial is wearing a killer form-fitting dress, perfect hair and make-up, high heels and looks like she just got home from her job...as maybe a hooker, or even maybe a secretary, it's hard to tell. Okay, kill me now. I couldn't wait to be the 24-hour woman!! This commercial actually said that!! So...the new vision of womanhood that I was seeing in mass media in 1980 included working 24 hours a day, looking sexy at work and then coming home, making dinner, and of course, having sex with your man after all of that! (Subliminal, but very implied) No problem! Okay, I was only 21 – so I thought, SURE I can do that. Bring it on. I have the energy and stamina and creativity for THAT plan.

Women were going to get executive jobs and executive pay and fame and fortune, wonderful husbands and amazing children and all of the stuff men have always gotten. And so, I believed all of that was possible. I was a kid. Yup. I know what you are thinking. Sure thing sweetie!! I will also admit to truly misguided feminist reading choices when I look back now. The "long repressed female aggressive literature" that appealed to me was an all or nothing; take no prisoners, kind of thinking. I do know now that life really doesn't work that way. But hey, I was 21. What on earth did I really know?

I was going to take over the world!! YAY!! I was going to do something...something...something big! YAY!! Women unite! Women are progressing! Or something like that. And then make dinner for my husband. No problem.

I literally marched out of college ready for the world and ready to embrace this new found "freedom" to have it all. I was a Phi Beta Kappa, Michigan State University graduate with high honors, recruited by Procter and Gamble. Ready, set go!!

My thinking was the following: – if I work hard enough, if I work long enough hours, if I really apply *"Games Your Mother Never Taught You"* to my work life, if I cut my hair short, if I wear a silk bow tie and carry a calculator, somehow I will be perceived as valuable as and as competent as my male counterparts. Even though I bet my male colleagues weren't asked about their marriage plans in their Procter and Gamble interview. Okay it WAS 1981. But really, go women? Hmmmm. Was I going to get married soon? Really...in my interview questions...

But then, I got a little older, a little wiser and started being promoted. Wow, I got my own office, I got more money. Wow!! Whee!! This stuff is really working! It made me a little dizzy. And the seduction of success and power pulled me in. Pulled Me In. Things had changed...somewhat. I was not a secretary. I was not an executive assistant. I was a MANAGER.

However, I mistakenly thought that things were changing *faster* than they really were. I mistakenly thought that if I "played like the boys" and only worried about making bonuses and profit and money (no soft, woman-like skills here), that I would be taken as seriously as the men. But it just never proved to be true. I believe that I was perhaps perceived more seriously than women of the previous generation. But I assumed an equality of thought and action that did not happen. Where did I go wrong? Whiny girl that I am.

Even if we decide that "playing like the boys" is how we will be taken more seriously, it remains a challenging concept for a woman to embrace for a couple of reasons that I can articulate.

Point #1: A big business shocker for me is that most MEN are also not perceived as competent by their companies, so women do not have any leg up (ha, ha) here. One of the weird advantages to being the only girl in the room is that you get to see how decisions are really made – very subjectively, personally, based on relational proximity (male loyalty) and perceived value. You also get to see how subjective everything truly is in these decisions. The myth is that men make decisions that are much more objective, non-personal, non-emotional and non-subjective than women. And that is just not true. That is just NOT true.

Point #2: The reason why "playing like the boys" can be challenging to make work is because business is all about making money and very little else. I have observed that the process of making this money can sometimes make people a little crazy - because everyone wants some of that money for themselves! ME!! MONEY!! MY MONEY!! The easiest thing in the world to do is to trust people who look like you, talk like you, act like you and think like you, which in most companies, is NOT a woman. It is much easier to trust a known quantity than an unknown quantity. Let's take the moral or cultural judgment off the table right now. It just is. So the men choose the men, because they have a level of implicit trust with them that is often not the case with women – at least in business situations.

My experience has not demonstrated that business is altruistic, focused on morals and equality and values and societal impact. My experience has shown me that business is about money and making money. There are many other institutions focused on these things including churches, schools, hospitals and even some government agencies. In my 30-year business career, I have not sat in rooms where I felt a whole lot of compassion floating around. I have felt anger, rage, greed, aggression and downright dishonesty. But not a whole lot of concern about diversity, balance, and perhaps – a clear assessment of real individual abilities and intentionally leveraging those abilities for the good of the organization.

I also feel like many of us in "my" generation did not get the "follow your dreams and the money will follow" memo, whether you were male OR female. I feel like work should be hard, difficult, you do whatever it takes to make the company happy, you take whatever happens and make the best of it, you put your head down and don't look up. If you are not happy, that is not even an issue because you are making good money, you have stability, you are working for a respectable company and you can support your family. End of story.

My father was born in 1926 and my mother in 1929, both in Nebraska. They were very, very smart, hardworking people. They taught me to value my intelligence and work hard. But I don't remember any conversations about doing something for a living that would make me happy, or doing something that would be fun for me and take advantage of my true strengths. I remember "respectability" being high on the list – working for well-known companies was good. High grades were good. And of course, stability and achieving a high salary was good.

I ended up in business vs. teaching or nursing or social work because it WAS a model that was not traditionally female and that was important to me. Procter and Gamble offered me a job. It was 1981, the economy in Michigan sucked and I was WANTED by a respectable company, with a respectable salary and a respectable company car. I don't know if it was really more complicated than that. Maybe if an educational institution had offered me a job I would still be in education. I would not say I brought a lot of highly creative thinking to my career. I made my parents proud, I have supported my family in ways that a woman 40 years ago would not have dreamed of, and I have been highly respectable. So, I guess I am supposed to be happy and grateful and stop whining. But I can't seem to do it!

Maybe my problem was starting to see and read more and more articles on how it IS possible to do something that doesn't drive you crazy, something that makes you happy, something that is your passion and makes you want to get out of bed in the morning. The "follow your passion and the money will come" movement. But I do remember thinking when I got out of college that the whole *What Color Is Your Parachute* idea was absolutely, self-indulgent, crap. Really? That is possible? Such a thing exists? WOW. I'm still mulling over that idea.

Business Wisdom Nugget #3: Business is ALWAYS highly subjective, personal, emotional, and often, very irrational. It has everything to do with making money. Which is personal. Very, very personal. People want to trust people who they understand and know. Men understand men in business. So they hire men. They hire women too. But they want as many men in the room as possible. And then maybe…you too. Keep praying….

4

ON BECOMING A MAN

If men choose men to be in power because they feel more comfortable around people who look and act like themselves, well then, I decided I was going to be more man-like. I was going to double-down on playing like the boys, experience-be-damned and get into the club! This idea involved the concept of me dressing exactly like my boss (the President of our Division) and the other senior executive counterpart at one of the companies on my double secret resume (you can view on LinkedIn) where I experienced some of my greatest business success. And my greatest business fun. But I thus digress.

Luckily, it was the 90's, so I didn't look too weird wearing white button down shirts under patterned men's cotton vests and black pants. My boss had a very expensive black car, so I got a less expensive black car. However, I did not cut my hair, after wearing short hair at Procter and Gamble, I went back to the classic "working women bob". I looked like a TV anchorwoman. Because my boss read *The Wall Street Journal*, I read *The Wall Street Journal*. But I do have to confess that I really, really like *The Wall Street Journal*. Let's be real here. *The Wall Street Journal* is *People Magazine* for business junkies. It's juicy and naughty and is considered so respectable and authoritative, but it is GOOD business gossip and innuendo. Business people are WAY crazier than entertainment stars. Just saying... I thus digress again!

And I was and confess I still am a business junkie and a student of business and knew every merger, transition and firing in the whole country. *The Wall Street Journal* was my business bible. I read it religiously every single day and always had something to say to my boss and male colleagues because I kept up. I was "hanging" with the boys. I dressed like my boss, I drove a cheaper but "like-type car" as my boss, I read the right newspapers and other business magazines just like my boss. And guess what? I was promoted! And given more money. So this plan was definitely working quite well. Maybe I had cracked the code after all. Yay!!

While I still wore make-up, curled my hair and wore perfume, there we were, the CEO, VP of Operations and the VP of Marketing, all wearing black pants and white button down shirts and patterned vests. We looked like the Mod Squad, for anyone who remembers that show. Two guys and a girl, except we had no diversity. We were all white. Which is also what corporate America looks like. Just saying. Two white guys and a girl. The girl is also white. That's often about as diverse as it got in the corporate world executive level ranks in the '90's.

In terms of the whole playing golf and sports thing, I drew the line. I have NEVER played golf. EVER. I will NEVER play golf. Even writing this now dates me. I don't think the 30-year-old women working for me today ever were told that they needed to play golf with the men to be successful. But I was. And that is the one thing I said no to in my business life. I do not play golf. When I am at an executive retreat and all of the men are signing up for golf foursomes, I very confidently sign up for the spa. Always. Even at Procter and Gamble. And it makes me very happy. I do not know why I choose NOT learning golf as the one business boundary I made, but I did. I do not even remember the decision process, but I made it. And I have never regretted it. And I have never caved in. I do not play golf.

However, I must confess that I have always tried to keep up with the hometown sports teams, or at least know what is going on at a high level. I also follow college football, specifically the Big 10, or 12 or 14 (who does the math on these things?) and my alma mater, Michigan State University. I did grow up bathed in Sunday NFL Football knowledge every week, courtesy of my father and brother, so I can talk about some of the older players (the Archie Manning Dynasty) and "nostalgia" stuff fairly easily. What is interesting to me is that sports conversations have changed dramatically over the many years of my work life. I know just as many women now who REALLY follow a sport and know everything about it as much as the men. This concept applies particularly to hockey in my current town of Chicago, IL. When I moved here in 1990, we all watched all of the Bulls games (of course the whole country watched the Bulls with Michael Jordan). Baseball as an overall sport seems to be more specialized, but I do always know what is going on at a high level with the Chicago Bears, even though I NEVER watch them, except if they are in the Super Bowl and I am at a party, sipping wine and pretending to care about the outcome!! Yay, go Bears!

And now, I actually know a lot of men who FREELY admit to not following sports at all in this day and age. And they do not seem ashamed or embarrassed. So that has been a very radical change over time in pre-meeting chit-chat and water-cooler conversations. Or really, broken copy machine conversations. As an aside, do copy machines ever really work? I have done entire deals while waiting for a copy machine to be fixed. Thank You. How can the people who designed these machines keep their jobs? If my business and marketing plans broke down as often as my copy machine, I would be fired far more frequently than every 5 years. Just saying....

In terms of physical appearance, I feel that over the past several years, the business expectation *has* transitioned to a fresher view point that it is OK if women look like women again, we don't need to look like knock-off clones of the men. (We don't need to don suits, ties, vests, pants, and adhere to, I guess you could say, a "de-feminization" of the female business work force). While I don't think that it is a bad idea to look like a woman at work, it does make things A LOT more complicated. Black pants are SO safe. A black jacket is SO safe. Why do you think Hillary Clinton wore pantsuits on the campaign trail? I can't knock her, once you start showing any skin - boob or leg, it can get complicated. What length is acceptable for a skirt? Can it be shorter if you wear black boots and black tights? How low of a neckline can you wear? Does it matter if you wear a big necklace to "fill in the space" around your neck? How about a low cut blouse with a scarf – is that OK if the scarf covers up any cleavage? Do men EVER have any of these thoughts about getting dressed for work? I really think that men never have to worry about exposing sexual parts of their body in their business dressing. Women Do.

A black pantsuit is the safest thing you can ever possibly wear.

I now wear black skirts and black stockings or black skirts and very thick black tights and pearls for every big meeting. LOTS of fake, big, pearls, both necklaces and bracelets and earrings and rings. And that seems to work out pretty well for this phase of my career. Or...sometime I will wear black jeans if I am interviewing at a venture capital digital start-up – or I will wear very tailored, designer blue-jeans if I am interviewing at a venture capital start-up in year 5. So easy to figure this all out!

However, I am very aware of the fact that many of the young women who work for me now seem to dress exactly the opposite of what I just discussed here. I see female colleagues walking around in skirts that are too short, low necklines with cleavage, lots of bare legs, high, high heels, and clunky jewelry. And while I think it is great and maybe even empowering to look like women at work, let's just remember we are NOT going clubbing. The middle ground is not a bad place to be. Right?

You cannot have your breasts exposed and command a room in a way that demands respect. You just can't. I can promise you that everyone WILL look at you. But they are looking at your breasts. I am still old-fashioned enough and corporate enough to think that the workplace is not "suited" for sexual distractions. And while I know lots of people who have met their husbands and wives at work, if this is going to happen, let's do this with a little more clothing in the picture. Not a bad thing at all. It's okay to leave something to the imagination. Thank You.

Business Wisdom Nugget #4: While it is not necessary at this point in time to dress like a man, it is very prudent to dress like you are NOT trying to pick-up your business colleagues... even if you are. Thank you. And your immediate boss will also thank you. Re-think what "appropriate" business attire means to you. And then ask for your mother's advice. Really. It might help.

5

A WORD, OR TWO, ABOUT THE "F" BOMB

Now, a word and business public service announcement about the "F" bomb. Yup. This chapter is about how to use the very volatile word "FUCK" in your career as a businesswoman in the best possible way. It is a very touchy subject! And fraught with many potholes and pitfalls along the way. When I started my career back in 1981, in the dark ages, I would say I experienced a bit more decorum around speech and speaking and swearing was fairly limited for BOTH sexes – or at least when both sexes were in the same room. I do remember moments when men would swear and then apologize to me when they happened to accidently notice that I was in the room, with a sheepish grin on their face. The implication was that it was OK to swear in front of other men, but not polite in front of a delicate and refined woman like me. So, certainly a double standard. I also felt, at the start of my career, that it would be unseemly for a woman to be caught swearing and saying, "fuck" around anyone. So.... I didn't. NEVER. EVER...THEN.

I really do think swearing is indicative of lazy language and lazy thinking and speech. There are so many other ways to express anger, frustration and disappointment in any situation. But there has always been swearing and there will always be swearing. And sometimes swearing gets the job done. Yup. Totally DONE. Especially in a business setting. And sometimes it is good to be efficient.

Maybe this is also specific to each company and environment. My last company was a total "F" bomb company and if you didn't drop one every now and then, you weren't in "the club". So consequently, my own speech has become somewhat lax on this word and I am now trying to rein it back in. But can I tell you there is something so powerful about a woman saying the "F" bomb that makes her seem tough, business-like and ready for action! And being seen as tough in the boardroom has never been a bad thing. So I must confess to liking the effect it has on a situation – if you use it *sparingly*. But there really are better ways than playing like the boys on this one. Rampant swearing and cursing does not indicate intelligence, power or authority in ANY situation. Male or Female. ALL of us can do better. It is just so easy!! FUCK! Let's look harder for ways to express frustration in ALL areas of our lives. Okay?? Okay. That blur you see power walking around the building parking lot is ME. And I'm not swearing!!

Business Wisdom Nugget #5: Swearing at work is a touchy subject. You need to evaluate your environment very carefully. But should you need to swear, saying the "F" bomb will get the attention you are looking for and silence the room immediately. However, this tactic needs to be used sparingly. Very. Sparingly. And maybe even, never.

6

THE CRYING GAME

As we were discussing the enormous workload expectations, the crazy office politics that I could not make go away and the sheer ridiculousness of the situation, she started crying. I automatically reached for the ever-present box of tissues in my office and made sure I had on my "sympathetic-looking" face.

In this job, almost every single person on my team had cried in my office. Yup, that would be BOTH the men and the women. I think this was a huge reflection on my inability to create a safe environment for my team and it made me mad. Not at them. But at the owners who created such a non-supportive place to work. I hate being out of control and I hate failing as a leader and it was obvious both were occurring quite regularly. Members of my team kept coming into my office and our discussion would end with tears, tissues and apologies. I don't mind someone crying in my office at all. And it does not make me think they are weak or ineffective or anything negative at all. In my experience, people who cry in the office are actually people who feel so passionately about what they do that they bring "all of themselves" to work. When things aren't going well, they hit the wall and their strong emotions come into play. Strong emotions are great things and I don't shy away from them at all WITH MY TEAM.

However, I have NEVER cried in front of a boss. EVER. Kind of like vomiting, I have always managed to "make it" to the bathroom, that cold and safe sanctuary of mine, the women's handicap stall at the far end of the bathroom, before I start crying.

If there was one message I got when I entered the workforce in 1981, it was DO NOT CRY. DO NOT CRY for any reason. It is the most "female" thing you could possibly do and would brand you for life as weak, not tough, vulnerable, not invincible, focused on the personal, not the

21

objective, and the bottom line is – MEN HATE WOMEN CRYING. At work. At home. Doesn't matter. DON'T CRY.

When women cry in their own personal lives with men, at least the men can pat them on the back, offer tissues, hug them and try to make all of that crying stop. When women cry at work, I can hear the fire alarms going off in my male colleagues minds, "Oh my God, she is crying, she needs to stop, what do I do, I can't touch her, what do I say, what can I do now to make this whole situation STOP. This is freaking me out!!!!" Men feel particularly out of control when a women colleague cries at work, especially if she is their subordinate. It overtly brings the personal aspect of a woman into the office, and emphasizes the gender differences, while we know we should always be objective and impersonal (yeah, right) and this crying stuff creates a horrendous amount of tension and unknown behavioral expectations. In all fairness, I really think women don't always feel comfortable with crying colleagues either, but for me personally, the personal, crossing over into the professional, crossing over into the overlap of the real person, does not make me uncomfortable. I have many fewer expectations about what is proper business behavior for my team, than for myself. As long as you do your job and can meet your goals, I will pretty much cover for you and whatever you do, crying included. Coming in late, leaving early, 2-hour lunches, whatever, do the job and I am YOUR boss.

So, what do I think happens when a woman cries in front of her boss? Because he feels out of control, he will definitely secretly hold it against you that you cried because you made him feel so uncomfortable. Because he never wants to feel that uncomfortable again at work, he is going to distance himself from you in small and large ways. This is only my belief based on my observations from watching other female colleagues.

The small ways include not sitting next to you in meetings, making sure that the two of you always meet in public spaces, his behavior becoming more guarded around you including joking with you less, and treating you like something that could, "go off", like a firecracker, at any moment. The large ways include not assigning you as the lead on big projects, not giving you the chance to present information in important meetings, and shutting you out of the major discussions held behind closed doors because he feels that have you have become a very tenuous colleague, and possibly "unpredictable."

These are just my observations, since I have never actually cried in front of a boss. But this seems fairly obvious – men don't cry at work a whole lot and I think the unspoken expectation is for EVERYONE to follow that rule – don't cry at work. It's kind of one of the last emotional taboos. While yelling is highly acceptable and anger is somewhat tolerated as long as violence is not involved, crying is… Really not so good.

Nope.

Good places to cry at work include, but are not limited to: the women's bathroom at work, an empty conference room, (as long as you keep the light off), your own office with the door securely LOCKED, your car in the parking lot at work, (but only if no one can see you), a colleague's office (one whom you can trust with your life) with the door shut, your car in a parking lot not at your place of employment and always, the safest place in the world, at your own home, in bed, with the covers pulled tightly over your head.

So while I recommend not traveling down the crying road at work, if it happens to you, shake it off and move on. Stuff happens. And maybe you will have a boss like me that doesn't care. She is too focused on feeling really bad and crappy about why you are crying and is not judging you at all, she is wondering why she is such a failure as a boss that she couldn't keep you from crying in your one-on-one update meeting with her that week. (I am hoping this book can fund more therapy…for ME).

Business Wisdom Nugget #6: Crying at work should be done privately, if you can manage it. If not, shrug it off, and maybe even make a joke about it. STILL not a good position to be in, sucking it up is probably easier for you and your boss. Sorry. Some things never change. Crying freaks everyone out. Remember <u>my</u> favorite hangout – the handicap stall in the women's bathroom. PERFECTION.

7

SHH... DON'T LET ANYONE KNOW, BUT I AM A MOTHER

I absolutely KNEW and FELT and READ that I should never let anyone know that I had "mother responsibilities", I knew I should never, ever, leave early for a school play, or a vomiting child, or a child in the emergency room. I was smart enough to lock my child out of my bedroom while she was banging on the door to take a Saturday afternoon conference call while all of the men in the room laughed and joked about how cute I was yelling at my daughter to be quiet. I spent a whole lot of time arguing with my husband over who had the most important job while we tried to figure out who was going to take care of our sick child. And then I KNEW that I should feel really, really horribly bad about all of this. But do it anyway. And...guess what? It worked!! I got promoted. Again. I got more money. I got more responsibility. YAY!!

This was probably the hardest part about becoming a man and playing like the boys. This was BEFORE it was really cool for guys to take off work to coach their kids baseball team, to see the school play, to go to the doctor's appointments. This was well BEFORE that phase – which I think is amazing and wonderful and wow, too bad it was after my time. I must admit to feeling somewhat jealous as my younger female colleagues take 12 weeks of FMLA for each child, go home early when needed and NEVER apologize for having children or being a mother. That is the way it should be. And I wish I could have experienced this new phase of the corporate world. Blah, I didn't feel any of "that".

But if you graduated college in 1981, my memories as a young mother include remembering the hard, cold feeling of that knot in my stomach I had on many, many days, waiting for daycare to call me in case a rogue fever broke out, waiting for a babysitter to call me because she was sick and couldn't pick up my daughter from school, waiting for the school to call me from the office with a sick child at the nurse's station. It was really, really tough. I felt like a crappy mother a whole lot of the time. Especially when I gave my kids Motrin before daycare, knowing they had a fever, but the Motrin would give me 5 hours at work before the dreaded call, once the fever popped out. Yeah, I was THAT mom. I put my kids in daycare, knowing they were sick, and trying to extend the time before I had to go home and be a Real Mom. Or something like that.

I just remember this very heavy feeling about not wanting to be seen as "soft", as the kind of business woman who always had to leave because of her children – that there was an implied weakness, an implied acknowledgment that I was different in negative ways from my male colleagues, that I could not be trusted with the same jobs and assignments because I "might have to leave to take care of my child."

This was especially sensitive around business travel. If you are a mother, can you travel? Can you go to those business meetings, those conferences and leave your kids home...with your HUSBAND? Because, gosh, can he really take care of those kids without you? Just because he is the father...can he really do it?

I stopped breast-feeding my son at 3 months old because I just did not have the energy to pump breast milk and take my first one-week business trip to New York at the same time. I just gave up. UNCLE.

I accepted this thinking and played like the boys. I probably regret this more than anything else in my career. I remember being gone on a few consecutive business trips during one summer when my kids were about 8 and 3 and when I got into the car at the airport, they made me sit in the back seat and they both grabbed an arm and wouldn't let go because they missed me so much. "Mommy, mommy, we are so glad you are home."

I personally also experienced a very subtle feeling of being a neglectful mother from my male business colleagues because I DID undertake business travel with young children at home. "You aren't going to that school concert? OH, your HUSBAND is going. Too bad."

One of the hardest and latest examples of me feeling torn was when I was away from home for several weeks to launch a new business and my high-school aged daughter came down with the Swine Flu. She called me as I sat my desk 800 miles away and was crying because she felt so crappy. I felt entirely helpless and out of control. Sometimes, you just feel very bad as a mom, no matter where you work – home or office. It's part of the job. And that is the dilemma – you can't be in the right place at the right time all of the time.

I don't care at this point what men really think about all of this, the way I played it was wrong and even though the workforce is different now because of LAWS, YAY for that. I know that men still find it a huge pain that we get pregnant and go on maternity leave, trust me, I have been in recent meetings where it was said, "yeah, but I think she lost her drive after she had her second child." BUT, the laws are helpful in giving us all a bit of a break. Of course, you need to work for a company that is large enough that they have to follow the family laws.

My daughter made me a beautiful Mother's Day card when she was about 4 years old. It was on pink construction paper and had a beautifully drawn flower on it. I still have it. Everyone thought it was so funny when she structured the card like a business memo: "To: Mom, From: Julia RE: I love you. Happy Mother's Day". Hard to know whether to laugh or cry.

When I was pregnant with my son, I waddled into the office, one week later than my "due date". I vividly remember feeling tired and depressed because I was supposed to have my son the *previous* Saturday. But…still no baby. I was huge. I was wearing one of two dresses that still fit me, and I felt fat and ready to be done with this pregnancy. It was a cloudy and cold Friday, November 22, and I was worried about trying to juggle and control several things as I started my work that day.

As I was walking thru the building in the morning, two male colleagues came up to me and said, "Are you still here?" – as if I was stretching out this pregnancy to annoy them with my largeness and lateness. The things people say to you, AT WORK, when you are pregnant are sometimes really annoying. It's as if we lose any semblance of respectability that we do have as businesswomen once we starting showing and our bellies are sticking out. You can feel the corporate tension in the air once a businesswoman is a pregnant. "OMG, how should we treat her? As a businesswoman, or as a pregnant woman?" This disconnect leads to comments like, "I can't believe how big you are!" from your male colleagues. What would be a comparable female to male comment about something going on with them physically? "My, my, John, your beer belly has grown to significant proportions and is hanging over your belt. Did you notice that?" Yea, right. Never happening.

My mind that Friday was spinning on overdrive, trying to figure out how to juggle my daughter's 5th birthday party at Chuck-E-Cheese for 30 of her kindergarten friends the next day and having this baby. The doctor wanted me to get another stress test on Saturday morning and the birthday party was set for noon. I didn't want to go into labor during my daughter's birthday party, I didn't want to be induced on Saturday after the birthday party and I was feeling like, yes, my children were already ganging up on me in the month of November, and one wasn't even here yet.

So I went into work that Friday morning, VERY fat, tired and worrying about my stress test the next morning that would indicate whether an induction, c-section or any other removal process was necessary to get the baby out. And I wanted nothing to get in the way of my daughter's 5th birthday party.

So…what happened next really blew my cover that not only was I already a mother, but I was going to be a mother again that very day. No more hiding out on this one.

We were in my boss'/mentor's office, having a meeting about our website. Those in attendance around the round table were all men; there were 5 of us all together.

I was NOT engaged with anything being said. I was bored and cranky and still trying to figure out this birthday party/having a baby dilemma in my head. I was looking at my watch. It was around 11:45 AM, right before lunch.

I am sitting at the table, trying to appear interested and all of a sudden I felt a familiar feeling. I moved around a bit in my chair, very inconspicuously, trying to determine what was happening. After a couple of minutes, I knew that my water broke.

My labor with my daughter also started with my water breaking. A very distinctive feeling indeed. Even though my doctor said that just because my water broke to start my labor with my daughter did not mean my water would break to begin my labor with my son… as any smart woman knows, you trust your gut on this stuff. So…I had brought into the office an old towel and had it my bottom desk drawer for the past month.

After I had confirmed in my head that my water broke, I remember feeling a great sense of relief and joy, since this meant I would be able to have my son BEFORE my daughter's birthday party since it was noon on Friday. The birthday party would go off without a hitch and I could have my son within the next 24 hours. Yay!! I love it when my plans fall together.

The best line I have uttered and will ever utter in a business meeting was mine for the taking. **"Hey, I hate to cut this meeting short guys, but my water just broke."**

BEST. LINE. EVER. EVER.

So, suddenly, I have 4 male colleagues starring at me in shock and awe. My boss says, "What would you like us to do?" And, of course, being the ever-prepared business executive that I am, replied, "why don't you leave the room and then I can walk back to my office."

Then I asked my boss' assistant to go ask my female manager to "get the towel." I had previously shown her where I was keeping it in my office cabinet in case of the "dreaded water breaking in the office possibility".

My male colleagues proceeded to flee the room, I think grateful that they weren't needed to be involved in the actual birth process, and my manager brought in the towel. I am so glad that I had the towel.

So she cleared the hallway of colleagues so that I could walk back to my office with a towel between my legs so I didn't mess up any of the carpeting or anything. What a moment in my business career! But I was so happy.

I then proceeded to sit at my desk with the towel between my legs and answer email for a while, knowing that I was going to have to be induced because that is what happened with my daughter and I was not having contractions. I knew the drill, doctor's directions to "come right to the hospital now" be damned. I wasn't going to have contractions until I got medically induced, so let's all take a chill pill.

Frightened and nervous business colleagues kept appearing at my office door, saying "Why are you still here, you should go home!" and then I finally finished up my email, feeling really, really happy that my plan was going to work out with my daughter having her birthday party at noon the next day.

I left the office around 1:00 PM, met my husband at home to get our stuff together, made sure my husband had our babysitter scheduled as back-up help on Saturday morning for the party and then finally left for the hospital.

At 7:05 PM, after only 4 hours of labor, my beautiful son was born, weighing in at 9 lbs. 3 ounces. My daughter's birthday party was perfect and she came over from the party with her birthday crown on, a balloon in her hand and a broad smile on her face to meet her new baby brother.

I gained a small amount of office fame for having my water break during a meeting. I must tell you, I am probably not that understanding sometimes when women on my team take off a week before their due date "to get ready for the baby." I do remind them that I almost had my son at work, in the middle of a meeting. (A little dramatic, but hey, not that far off) Working in the corporate world for over 30 years has rubbed off on me a little bit and sometimes I can be a pain in the ass too. Yup. Sorry!

Business Wisdom Nugget #7: Don't pretend you are not a mom. Don't pretend you are not a business WOMAN. The two roles can co-exist. Hang tough on this one. And ALWAYS choose your children first. The job is <u>not</u> your legacy. And it never hurts to keep a towel in your bottom desk drawer.

8

THE PROBLEM IS <u>NOT</u> MEN

This might seem to be a strange statement to make when you think about what I have just written in the previous chapters. But my up and down business career has introduced me to some of the funniest, smartest, most creative, caring, nicest men on the planet. I have very close male friends that I have made at every job I have ever had. I love, love, love them. And those include men who graduated BEFORE 1981 – so as I like to tease them, the true dark ages of business, men and women working together.

Some of my biggest supporters, champions and encouragers in the business world have been and are men. My one mentor in my business life is a man.

In 1990 I walked into his office for an informational job interview and my business life changed forever. Seriously. You don't know when you first meet someone that they are going to be your mentor and change your entire life. It starts out as just another meeting, or interview or conversation. The business books all say you need a mentor, or at least did in those days. And maybe everyone does need one, but the mentor/protégé relationship is not without it's own issues either. And it's NOT as easy as finding a job.

In the 80's and 90's, the business wisdom was all about "going out and networking to find a mentor." I would attend various business association lunches and dinners, I would talk to everyone I could meet and studiously exchange my business cards. And after awhile, I rightly concluded that you can't "shop" for a business mentor any more than you can "shop" for a friend. It either happens or it doesn't. There is definitely some magic and chemistry involved and you cannot manufacture that in a relationship. If you are fortunate enough to have a mentor, I suggest you treasure that relationship. Mentors don't come along every day in every job. I think most of us can only find one, if we are very lucky. Kind of like a soul mate.

My mentor is an entrepreneur, a risk-taker, a high energy, and very engaging, charismatic man. He is positive and creative and listens well. He reads and thinks and is always willing to learn something new. He is seriously one of the most interesting people that I know. He is brilliant at business. He is funny and caring and totally loves his wife and kids. He has his priorities right. I have NEVER seen him yell at anyone. I have seen him frustrated and disappointed and mad. Even at me. We even had a major falling out, really like a business break-up if you will. And then we got back together again. Which made everyone we worked with much happier. And of course, me too.

He has always been honest with me. He has encouraged me to do things I really thought I could never do. He believes in me in a crazy sort of way. We can sit and talk business stuff and life stuff for hours. We have always liked the same books, movies and TV shows. He pushes me. He makes me believe in myself in ways I never thought possible. He really makes me a better me. And I am not writing a greeting card right now!

But that is what a good mentor can do for you. They make you believe you can do really big things and then they encourage you and then you end up doing things you really couldn't do on your own steam. I didn't ever want to disappoint him. So I worked like crazy to always do my best. And it has paid off in my whole career so far. The absolute biggest business blessing of my life.

I myself am a mentor to a woman who has worked for me three times in her career so far. It has been an amazing and unpredictable journey over the past 23 years. Being a mentor has been a good and wonderful experience for me because it has helped me understand some of the challenges I have had in the past with my own mentor. I have not always been pleased with my protégés performance. We have had tough conversations. But we have never given up and I am extremely proud of her. She has gained skills and achieved knowledge that has surprised me. I sometimes underestimated her. And I think her career is in a better place because of our relationship. I am a better businesswoman because of her. She pushes me to be a better boss and mentor myself. And for that, I am eternally grateful. We are also best friends. Not everyone can pull off the business/friend thing and set good boundaries. But we have done a pretty good job over the past 2 decades, fluidly going back and forth between the business-friend roles. And the advantage of that is working with someone you trust completely, like and like being around for 24 hours a day. It makes everything at work just that much better. A total business blessing.

But I need to caution you to remember, if you end up in a mentor/protégé relationship, it is a RELATIONSHIP. There will be ups and downs. My huge down with my own mentor came when I got promoted into a job where I didn't report directly to him anymore. It was in the "up and coming division." And the CEO decided to sell the division my mentor was President of and actually founded himself. On paper, for me, this was a big YAY! But, let me tell you, we were both feeling highly uncertain, threatened by all of the changes and we did not handle this situation well at all. We actually fought in meetings in front of the CEO. It was absolutely horrible. I felt sick and depressed. It was a nightmare. He actually tried to get me fired. My stomach hurt every day. It was so strange for me because it was totally unexpected. I didn't anticipate that all of this change would really change our relationship – or at least change how we would relate to each other. Now I can look back and see the huge warning signs that of course these changes were going to have a BIG impact on everyone. I can also now look back and understand how wrenching it had to be for him as his "baby", his company, was practically being sold out from under him.

Thankfully, another executive intervened on my behalf (a man) with the CEO and said we were both behaving badly and he would tell us to knock it off and take care of it. I am forever grateful to him. FOREVER. We needed a mediator and he was the perfect person for that job because we both trusted him enough to listen to him and do what he said.

As I think about these types of relationships, I have discovered that when your protégé starts to do REALLY well, and maybe start coming close to your own abilities, skill sets and position within the company, it feels really weird. Uncomfortable. Threatening. Scary. It is totally irrational for the most part, and I absolutely, positively hated feeling that way, but when I felt threatened when my own protégé was moving right along, I started to understand how my mentor probably felt when I was promoted.

If you are a mentor, do not try to squash your protégé just so you can feel better. RESIST. Go have a drink. Do something. Talk to someone about how crazy jealous you are feeling. Talk to someone about how you are mad at your protégé. Talk to someone about how you are losing your mind. Do not dump on your protégé.

The very good news is that the crazy, out-of-control feeling does pass. I want my protégé to go as far and as high as she possibly can. My mentor and I reclaimed our relationship after our fiasco and I actually ended up working for him again at another company. We remain, to this day, amazingly great friends. Interestingly enough, my mentor and my protégé have the same birthday, November 30th. Sweet.

Again, some of my biggest supporters, champions and encouragers in the business world have been men. My career would not have been possible without the support of my first husband. Even when he became my ex-husband.

I want to go on record saying that my first marriage did not end because I worked. I cannot be more emphatic about that idea. I could not have been successful in my career without him, his support and his willingness to co-parent with me during AND after our marriage.

I don't know how any woman can become successful without the support of her partner, especially if she is a parent. You cannot do it all. You just can't. And yes, while my ex-husband and I had our "stare down" times about who was going to take off work to care for a sick child, I probably won more of those face-offs. He stayed home A LOT.

And when I traveled, which was also often a lot, my husband/ex-husband was at home, not "babysitting" our children, but caring for them, as any good father would do.

Without my MALE mentor and my MALE husband, I would not be where I am today. The challenges in my career are not just because of men.

Business Wisdom Nugget #8: The reason why the corporate world is so difficult and unfair is not simply because there are a lot of men in it. The business model is fairly unforgiving for all sexes. And if you find an actual business mentor, value that relationship and experience – and consider paying it forward yourself. It's worth it. Trust me.

9

THE SOLUTION IS <u>NOT</u> WOMEN

Even though men have been part of many of the fundamental problems in my career challenges, (despite the good ones that I just discussed), I also discovered in my journey that the solution is NOT women. This was a surprising and profoundly depressing discovery. I thought that if I worked for a woman and worked with more women, everything would work out great! Women unite! Women are nicer than men, women understand how hard it is to be a business person and wife and mother and daughter. Women are kinder and gentler souls. Women are better listeners. Women are harder workers and are more focused. Women are the answer!!

WRONG. Did I say, "wrong"?

I got a sketchy performance review by my woman boss, who was under the woman CEO and it was totally ridiculous, mainly because the CEO was simply dreadful, really, and trying to manage HER was a full time job for everyone.

My performance feedback included a discussion of how I should NEVER ask the female CEO to repeat a directive while I was taking notes. Seriously. It made her mad. So somehow, I, as the VP of Marketing, was apparently not writing fast enough in our meetings and I was being chastised for asking the CEO to repeat herself. It made my head swim.

Women in BUSINESS, who make it to the top, have done all of the things I have outlined here, so in essence, they have become like men. Only worried about money, profit and getting money for themselves. So it doesn't feel any different at all or make my life any easier at all working for a woman. At least in the timeframe of my career.

And it becomes disappointing, possibly because my expectations when I had women CEO's were so radically different. Probably unrealistically so, I admit.

When I think about those experiences – of mainly women in the key executive roles, including the CEO, I am left to wonder about power and business and do we not all adopt the same pattern, at least in my generation, for what "authority" looks like? Does it always look male, controlling and autocratic, EVEN if you are female? Or does it always look male, controlling and autocratic just because that is what a CEO looks like, if you are a baby boomer or older? Will all CEO's going forward look male, controlling and autocratic regardless of their sex, age or race because that is what is needed to be a successful CEO? I wonder....

I have been a female "boss" since I was 26 years old. I have had a whole lot of people work for me in 29 years. I don't know if the men felt weird about working for me. I don't know if the women felt weird about working for me. I never really thought about it, because I was focused on meeting objectives, building great teams and building into my teams. As much as I am conscious of my gender in the boardroom, I am NOT conscious of my gender with my teams. I don't know what that means, but I always feel very comfortable being a leader with my immediate team – I never feel marginalized, or not enough or too female. I have always felt "just right". I'm sure that has kept me going through many of the other challenging moments.

When I think myself as a "boss", I don't really think about gender. I am thinking about impact and relationships and how can we structure ourselves to be successful? How can we also have fun?

Are the two "female" words in above sentence "relationships" and "we"? Don't know. I have ALWAYS had the highest performing teams in the companies I have worked. I have never felt that anyone on my team had a problem with me being a woman. EVER. Maybe I ignored it? Maybe they hid it? I don't know. It is interesting, but I never frame any of my thoughts, actions or behaviors through the filter of "girl" with my working teams.

Having a woman CEO and women executives in key positions who are above 40 years old didn't change anything. But it did provide me with the one experience where I walked into the women's bathroom one fine day and had a rather long conversation with the CEO in her bra, slip and pantyhose, curling her hair before an evening event. She was wearing nice lingerie, I must say. And I did keep my composure while trying not to think about talking to the CEO in her underwear.

I know men run into their bosses in the men's room all of the time, but it doesn't really happen that often for us women. That is one place we can usually go to escape the CEO. And the woman CEO at one of my companies had her own bathroom off of her office, so we never ran into her while freshening up.

So...again, women aren't the solution. Sigh.

Business Wisdom Nugget #9: There is no correct gender selection to finding a great boss, a great CEO or a great manager. Male or female, if only it were that easy, why is everyone so darn crazy at the top? There must not be enough air up there to keep anyone stable.

10

TOO

"Nancy, I know you are trying to effect change and progress, but you are seen as a bull in a china closet. I have gotten complaints about you. You need to tone it way down." Thus said my boss to me, about 6 weeks after my promotion to a manager position in my first really "important" job. I was 26. He was smoking a pipe, back when you could smoke in the office and I was very attentively sitting in a chair next to his desk.

My immediate response was to nod obediently and then go home and burst into tears and sob for a really long time. A bull in a china closet? That is a really bad image. It made me feel horrible. Why was I a bull in a china closet? Because I wanted to get things done? Would he have said that to man? Really? I was driven, focused and wanted to move the department ahead. A bull in a china closet? I am 5'10", so not a small woman by any means and this comment struck home on many levels.

What was I breaking? The old status quo? After some thought and reflection, I figured out that the "complaints" had come from.... another woman, who felt threatened by my promotion.

What a horrible and demoralizing thing to say to your new manager who is only 26 years old. I am a bull? Give me a break. I am a girl and you want me to be good and docile and calm. Yup. I get the message. Point taken. Or I HEAR this message: I was a bad girl and I need to be a good girl. Good girls don't make trouble, or make people feel uncomfortable or do whatever else I managed to do in just 6 short weeks as a new, untrained, manager. My first management feedback in my first management position. Click. File.

"The talk" has continued throughout my entire career. I have been told countless times that I am TOO assertive, TOO aggressive, TOO loud, I have TOO many opinions, I laugh TOO much and TOO loudly, I am TOO negative; I am TOO positive, I am TOO hard on my team, I am

36

TOO soft on my team, I am TOO detailed-oriented, I am TOO hands off, I am just "TOO".

I really think this type of feedback is not given to men. The content might be the same, but I truly believe that men are asked to make behavior changes at work in ways which involve feedback that is far less PERSONAL and demeaning. I also think that the word "TOO" is very much a word that is used with only female behavior and not male behavior in the business world. Like Sheryl Sandberg states in *Lean In*, no man is EVER told that they are "bossy." Men, have an inherent right to be the boss. Most women have been told that they are "bossy" at some point in their lives.

Okay, I hear you. I am just not "right". And working in environments where I am not right has been the biggest drain on my self-esteem I have ever encountered. My reaction is always to try and course correct by becoming "less". If I am "too" and that is BAD, than if I become "less", maybe that will get me back in the good graces of the company. And it is truly hard for me to believe that any company benefits by all of its female employees keeping a check and balance on their true natures and striving to be LESS of who they need to be. Seriously, can you really laugh too loudly? NOT really!!

Business Wisdom Nugget #10: The feedback you receive as a woman is tremendously different from the feedback you receive as a man. There is no rational way to deal with this difference that is not threatening to your supervisor. So just deal. And don't compare your "year end review" notes with your male colleagues or you will be very, very upset. Yup. I'm just saying...I bet he wasn't told to smile more in meetings.

11

I AM A HUMAN FIREWALL

"Could everyone who is competing in the *3rd Annual Screaming Flying Monkeys Contest* please report to the Marketing Roundtable area? The contest begins at 2:00 PM. Thank you." I got off of the company-wide speakerphone and went back to my desk to get prepared for the contest.

Everyone on my team came running with their *Screaming Flying Monkey* slingshot. Some participants had been practicing their shooting form earlier in the day and earlier in the week. The flying monkey's made a very loud and obnoxious screaming, wailing sound on being launched down the hallway. REALLY LOUD. EEEEEEEEEEEE!!!!

The monkeys originally came into the team through the creative thinking of the photography manager. He brought a few in one day to show me and I demanded that we order one for everyone on the team. THEN, I decided we needed to have a contest to see who could shoot their monkey the farthest down our marketing hallway. We marked the monkey landings with yellow post-it notes on the floor and on the sides of the cabinets. Shooting and controlling your Screaming Monkey was not as easy as it looked. It took some skill...really.

The contest was held during December, on the Friday before Christmas, one of the most stressful times of the year for our business. Everyone needed a chance to let off a little steam and this was the perfect way to do that. I also LOVED it.

The trophy was a white elephant gift I had received at another Christmas party. It was a truly frightening and strange metal sculpture of a tin woodman-type soldier on a horse, all done in colored metal on a stand. It was...simply horrendous, and therefore, perfect for the winning prize. The prize had resided on the cabinet of the 2nd year winner for the past 12 months and it was time to pass the torch! Ready, set go!

After 30 minutes of intense and very loud competition that not only included the noise from the screaming monkeys, but just an enormous amount of trash talk among the team members to each other, the photography manager who had originally found and brought us the monkeys actually won that year! He was awarded the wonderful metal prize, sadly given to him from the previous year's winner and another *Screaming Flying Monkey Contest* was in the history books. Laughter and fun! At work! Really! YAY!

I must confess, I am obsessed with making people laugh and with having fun at work to bring my team together, to make the day go faster and to put our stresses in perspective. Humor at work is not easy to orchestrate and navigate as a boss. You need to understand that you are playing with fire and be brave enough to handle the flying sparks. It can derail very easily. I have been fortunate enough not to have any truly bad incidents occur though all of my humorous antics.

I would suggest acquiring a certain amount courage and bravery to be funny as a boss. You need to edit out of your head all of those strange and random thoughts that can be a roadblock to humor in the workplace. "I won't be taken seriously by my team, we have serious work to do, we can't be seen sitting around laughing all day long, my boss won't like it, I don't want to get into trouble for making fun of people, we have so many HR policies I don't even know what I could joke about, this feels really SCARY……". Okay. That's fine. Do it ANYWAY. I dare ya.

Rule #1: You can never put anything in writing that you aren't totally comfortable with ANYONE reading out loud in a staff meeting. Including YOUR boss. Seriously. A whole lot of my humor is usually directed at myself for this very reason.

Rule #2: You need to truly KNOW your team.

Rule #3: You need to have TRUST. And that is why you can't walk into a new job and start immediately joking around with folks. Humor takes trust and that is built over time. No other way around it. Time and trust. Tread carefully until you know you have it.

I have written dozens of David Letterman-like "Top 10 Lists" and sent them to the entire team. They have been focused on current work specific situations that may have been somewhat stressful and tense. Or not. Nothing makes me happier than hearing the loud and spontaneous laughter echoing down the hallway when someone on my team opens these emails. It really makes my day complete.

I have kicked off and supported "word of the day" contests. Someone on the team is assigned the task of sending around a word definition each morning and then everyone has to email the team back a sentence with that word in it. Of course, the more clever and witty and maybe jabbing to another team member, THE BETTER. Game on!! It's at most a five-minute exercise that puts everyone in a great mood. Especially on a Monday morning, not a bad thing at all.

I hosted Friday afternoon drinks and snacks at 4:30 PM and had a whole lot of my team hanging out, talking and laughing until 7:00 PM on a Friday. A lot.

Our HR department required us to engage in numerous online training classes. One of the classes that was required for everyone to take was an online Internet safety and security class. It was 90 minutes of sheer educational torture and boredom, interspersed with online tests. The theme, *"I Am A Human Firewall"* had me heading for the humorous emails big time. I was close to creating "I Am A Human Firewall" T-Shirt for my team, but I got distracted and ended up having a gathering of Friday afternoon drinks and snacks instead. That was WAY more fun anyway. But I would often say, "I Am A Human Firewall" to distract the team and get a cheap laugh.

I feel very strongly about the power of fun and humor at work. And actually, in life. It helps if humor is like a religion for you, which it is for me. I adore creating humorous commentary on everyday boring things. Done right, it is one of the best ways to meld a team together and create loyalty to one another. And also make your team really productive. And there is nothing, nothing better, than belly laughing with the people with whom you spend 10 hours a day in your work life. It is the BEST high ever. I feel SO GOOD after laughing. And for me personally, I know that I set the tone for the team. If everyone sees that I have a sense of humor, then they can also relax and participate in the fun. And also create fun themselves. YES!!!!

Business Wisdom Nugget #11: Don't ever underestimate the power of your work team laughing together. Again, you always need to remember that you are playing with fire, so you must never demean anyone, you need to know where the pain points are and you need to have a solid sense of the different personalities of your employees.

12

THAT WAS THEN, THIS IS NOW

We moved to Kalamazoo, Michigan in March of my 1st grade year from Western Springs, Illinois. My dad had just landed a plum research job with *The Upjohn Company,* a prestigious, family-owned pharmaceutical company. The moving vans backed up to the door, we packed up, got into our car and drove to Kalamazoo, Michigan. I was excited and scared at the same time. Everything was new!

My mother often said that starting at Upjohn was like achieving the American Dream. Upjohn "owned" Kalamazoo in a way – buildings and foundations were already called "Upjohn", it was not especially easy getting a job at The Upjohn Company, it was somewhat of a big deal, and my mother felt that people in general treated you differently when they found out you worked at Upjohn. They treated you better. "Aahh, you work at *Upjohn."*

When my parents were looking to buy a new home in Kalamazoo, their realtor started showing them a different type of house when they found out my dad worked at Upjohn. My parents bought a brand new 4-bedroom home in a brand new up-and-coming neighborhood, one block from the best elementary school in the city. (According to my teacher mother, she did all of the research of where we should live, and deemed "Winchell Elementary School" the best in Kalamazoo. So that's where we lived!).

My mother often commented on how bad she felt for me as the economy and the work landscape started changing. My father had a pension. My father had Upjohn stock. My father had Upjohn bonuses. My father had Upjohn medical insurance. My parents did not save for retirement. My parents did not save for my college career. For college, they cashed out Upjohn stock, for retirement they lived on my dad's Upjohn pension and had amazing medical insurance. My father was taken care of by Upjohn. The Upjohn family had a stake in Kalamazoo, a long and deep reputation in the community to uphold, and the city was enormously better off for the Upjohn family. My parents died with no debt, money in the bank – not a fortune, but I never paid anything for my mother's 7 years of intense medical care before she died of emphysema, courtesy of my father's insurance. My father, having worked for Upjohn, was a very fortunate man and our family was also very fortunate because of their business policies.

My impression from closely watching my father's career was that you worked hard and were loyal and "the company" responded in kind. I truly think this was a good thing, for the employees, their families and the community. Upjohn was able to attract some of the best scientists in the country. Our community was diverse, intelligent, cultural, educated and expanding. In large part BECAUSE of The Upjohn Company, Kalamazoo, Michigan was not just another insulated, small town with a funny name. The company AND family gave back, they invested in the community and the company and everyone seemed to win.

This post-World War II business construct started to crumble right when I hit the work force in 1981. Because of increasing competition, both domestically and internationally, combined with tough domestic economic forces, the age of the large, prosperous, family-controlled company started changing. As mergers, buyouts and acquisitions started occurring, the "family" left the company and all bets were off. Apparently, no one could afford what had previously transpired. Apparently, not one CEO could figure out how to pay and treat employees in a fair fashion without tanking the company. This change happened almost overnight. There was no "step down" or transition period, people became dispensable and not seen as contributing to the bottom line, only the expense line. This was very bad and knee-jerk business thinking. The idea that your employees were a good and leverageable resource went away. I was told upon launching my career in 1981, to remember, "you can always be replaced." I cannot even communicate my thoughts on the idiocy of this comment. Our country created the economic disaster of 2008 without any outside help based on these ideas. The "every man for himself" business philosophy has been producing diminishing returns for the past 20 years in my opinion. Growing through cutting is not a strategy. It is a defense. Where are the "new products, old products with better margins, new customers and getting existing customers to return" strategies?

No one had any "skin in the game." The new "short term thinking game" for public company CEO's – if you are brought in as a CEO with a certain financial package and certain targets, you only care about hitting those numbers and moving on. We were slowly losing the idea of investing in the community where you were headquartered. What happened to investing in your employees? What happened to realizing that talented and well-trained employees produce profits? Oh!!! I remember. Let's cut overhead, let's cut our operational costs and we are profitable! It's hard for me to believe how quickly this change in thinking happened without any demonstrated research.

Companies were profitable, but NOT because they were creating products and services. They were profitable because they were cutting benefits, overhead, margin and talent. That works for a short amount of time, but it is not the silver bullet.

As CEO's and employees started working and thinking as "business mercenaries", innovation, growth and creativity suffered mightily. As I drive by my mall and see Bakers Square closed, Lowes closed, Circuit City closed, Blockbuster Video closed, Kmart closed, it's a retail and brand-name morgue of lost vision, as well as of shifts in retail and consumer demand that all of the boys in the room couldn't fix or solve.

All of THIS…did not help the cause of integrating the workforce from a gender or race standpoint. I think it further polarized the two factions of "boys" trying to run things and us "girls and minorities" trying to get in. It is still a strong force to this day. Major national brands are involved in HUGE layoffs and downsizing of their organizations. Can we just deny that this is NOT a small reflection on our ability to leverage our resources here in this country? Are we really not smart enough to figure out the profitability equation, because we are overextended as a culture? Or are we really not as smart as the competition?

It is impossible to ignore that all of these moving pieces did not affect women getting into "the room." It prevented many people from getting into "the room", and also people who could have helped these companies climb out of the ditch. What a huge waste of talent.

My mother had an old-fashioned phrase, "Don't throw out the baby with the bathwater." The underlying meaning and message was that while the bath water was probably dirty after the baby's bath, the baby was worth keeping! So don't go overboard in your reaction/correction/response to something because you may make decisions that are TOO drastic and TOO final and you end up throwing out the GOOD with the BAD. Don't throw out the precious baby!!

I am going to go on record and say that YOU are not replaceable. Really. You CANNOT be replaced. I have never hired a "commodity" in my entire career. I hire amazing PEOPLE who do amazing things because of who THEY are. These PEOPLE have deep skills, want to continually learn and want the company to be successful. These PEOPLE want everyone to win. "That other person" could NOT DO WHAT THEY DO. Okay? So, let's get over the antiquated idea that PEOPLE are not needed for the success of the company. The RIGHT people make all of the difference in the world. ALWAYS.

Business Wisdom Nugget #12: EVERYTHING has changed in business in the past 30 years. You do need to be your own best advocate and cheerleader in your corporate career, because no one is going to take on that task for you. The challenge is to be as selfish as you need to be to protect yourself and as supportive as you need to be to truly support good teammates and colleagues. But remember...no one is looking out for your best interests except for YOU.

13

MY MOTHER

My mother was born in 1929 in a small town in Nebraska. She unfortunately was born somewhat too early to be as ambitious as she was. She was very, very smart, the high school valedictorian, and the college valedictorian, Miss "Straight A Student". She was always very proud of her academic accomplishments. She went into education and teaching because it seemed more achievable and reasonable than being a journalist, which had really grabbed her interest. I think she would have been a great businesswoman. But, I also think the spark got blown out of my mother when she didn't go back to work after she had my brother and me. She actually wasn't a great housewife. I think she was bored and very lonely and under-stimulated intellectually. But she loved teaching. Especially teaching special education students, or students with learning disabilities or gifted students. She loved the challenging students, which is why I think she would have been so good in business. My mother loved a full-on challenge.

Because my father had a solid career, my mother didn't "have to" work and told me that it looked bad if you worked when your husband could support you. That was her perception. I know many women worked in the 1960's and 1970's but, as I biked around my neighborhood in the warm and lazy summers of my youth, I couldn't point to any mom that worked in business or outside the home, so I think she had a point. My mother was also somewhat obsessed about appearances and what other people thought. So, while ambitious, and also very competitive, not a real trailblazer. They don't always go together.

My mother died when I was 34 and she was 64. My daughter was 18 months old. It changed everything about my life to this day, some things for the good, some things for the bad. She was a life-long chain smoker and had emphysema. She did not live long enough to see my first promotion to Vice-President of a company. She did not live long enough to see me start a new business from the ground up. She also did not live long enough to see my deep frustration with my career, my struggle with balancing the demands of a job and the two kids and the husband and the volunteer work. She missed the part where I was functioning under a cloud of total exhaustion most of the day.

So while I adored my mother and always listened to her advice, she was a woman of two minds. She was a very smart businesswoman who didn't work in business but who would "steal" *The Wall Street Journal* out of my father's briefcase every day. She was a very smart businesswoman who didn't work in business but gave me very smart business advice. She was a very smart businesswoman who didn't work in business but gave my dad great business advice. She was a woman born in 1929 and had other pieces of advice that I ignored, but sometimes experienced as a painful reality anyway. She was honest, I will give her that. Honesty coming out of her own experiences and times.

So here are some truisms that I heard from my mother:

Men don't like women who are taller than they are. (I was 5'9" in junior high, ending up at 5'10 ½")

Men don't like women who are TOO smart; so don't show off your knowledge. (So much for MY own straight "A's")

Men don't like women who are TOO funny. (I am a jokester, just like my dad)

Men don't like women who are TOO loud. (I am not a soft speaker)

Men don't like women who are TOO ambitious. (So much for that last promotion of mine)

Don't ever be in a position where you need a man to support you, because they could leave you. Always be able to support yourself. (Okay, I probably really need a career)

Having children is the best thing you could ever do. (Okay, I need a man at least for PART of that equation)

Don't trust your women friends to tell you the truth because they could just be trying to steal your boyfriend or husband. (I often did not have a husband or boyfriend, so I have trusted my women friends implicitly my whole life without ever regretting it.)

You can never really be truly "friends with men" because they really, secretly, all want to date you or have you as their girlfriend. (In spite of the amazing rant in the middle of "When Harry Met Sally" about this, I have had male FRIENDS my WHOLE life who were supportive and loving and kind and amazing and NONE of them ever came on to me. So I am either really super repulsive, or men are able to be friends with women even though they are married, dating or gay. OKAY??)

So the double message I got from my mother – you can do anything you want to do, you need to get good grades, you need to strive for a great career, it's great for you to be funny and conquer the world! Oh, but, by the way, men don't like any of those things so you won't get a man that way.

I found all of this "wisdom" quite confusing actually. Almost everything that I was, everything that my mother wanted me to be, would put me at odds with having a relationship, getting married or having kids. I WANTED to get married and have kids and work too. I never envisioned a life of work only, even though I really wanted to do some exciting things in my career life. So, I navigated my way through this myriad of conflicting ideas by ignoring the "what men like part" and worked on just being myself in most situations, which has worked out OKAY in my social life. I have gotten married twice and have two wonderful children, but certainly feel like some of this advice did apply to my work life.

All of the "too" stuff my mother told me about has come back to haunt me at some point in my professional life. If I created a profile from her list, I don't think a man who was "tall, ambitious, funny, somewhat loud, career-minded with children" would be deemed "a problem" by other men. Or other women.

Having my mother as my mentor for my professional life that was just getting started when she died would have been a very interesting journey. I think she would be proud of me. And what I accomplished. She certainly would be proud of her granddaughter who is a commercial airline pilot. I never told my daughter she was TOO anything, accept maybe strong-willed. But don't we want our pilots to be strong-willed? Yup. Fly that plane!

Business Wisdom Nugget #13: Honor your father and mother, but realize that sometimes their thoughts and ideas are not always that helpful. Their experiences and your experiences are going to be different. However, be aware that if even if you don't agree with their advice, it keeps ringing in your own ears for years to come. Yup, that's called ...therapy.

14

MY GUILTY SECRET

I vividly remember my brand new dress, my black and white saddle shoes that I didn't know how to tie by myself, even though my mother tried very hard to teach me that skill, the big piano in the corner of the room, lots of kids running around and walking through the door and not looking back. It was the best day of my life. It was the first day of Kindergarten. I was blissfully happy. Really. I was in heaven.

I LOVED school. From day one. I loved everything about school. I loved the learning and the teachers and the classmates and the activities. I loved sitting in the front row of the classroom and I raised my hand for every question. I was not a big fan of summer vacation and time off because there was no school. I loved every September and Labor Day and the start of a brand new school year.

I loved being first, best, smart, I loved getting good grades, I loved doing well on tests, I just loved it all. I loved being singled out, I loved getting the flute solo in the junior high band, I loved having my paper read out loud to the class in 9th grade because it was deemed "so good" by the teacher. I loved my teachers; I loved the competitiveness of the environment, I loved school in a crazy sort of way.

As I look back on my up and down work life, I find myself needing to admit that as much as I loved school, as much as I loved everything about my first day of Kindergarten, I have spent a great deal of my career absolutely, positively, LOVING being **the only girl in the room**. Yup. I am the special one. I am the only girl with all the guys. I am the one that has "made it" into "that room". Being in the room, especially when you are the only one, signifies your specialness, your worthiness, and your significance. I am here and you are not. I get to sit in the first row and get called on when I raise my hand. Naa, na, na, na naa!

It's a feeling not unlike that from my mother's conflicting advice. I really did not think I would be the only girl in the room when I started my career. I was surrounded by other ambitious women, we were all starting out together and I never thought about spending so much of my career as the only girl surrounded by the guys. I never thought about being special because of my gender, I was originally motivated to be different and prove myself because of my skills and abilities.

But as time went on, I would be in the room and look around, and realize I was the only girl. More times than I care to admit, rather than be appalled by this fact, I turned it into something positive, just for me. And it really wasn't about me. It was about the fact that there really were not going to be many girls in that room, no matter how talented you were. We needed to make money, we needed to make our bonuses and the room was very comfortably filled with most people who looked like each other. Other white men.

It has taken me a very long time to realize what is WRONG with being the only girl in the room. What is wrong is that we are leaving out a very large talent base that is crucial for business success. WOMEN. We are leaving out new thinking and ideas and creativity just to maintain a secure status quo. WOMEN. And I think that it is hard to bring this up because those of us who have gotten into the room know that if we cause too much of a fuss, we will be kicked out. Seriously. And since all of us women who are in the room secretly like being in the room, we are only going to cause "so much trouble". We behave like "good girls" so that we can keep our seat and status at the big table. Guilty. As charged!

One of my team members said to me at my last job that I was the toughest person that he knew. He said this statement as a full-on compliment and I initially took it as a compliment. But really, why does anyone have to be "that tough" to succeed in business? Most businesses are about making things and selling things – not launching a full-on battle or war. I have sold diapers and movies and office products and cookware and gift baskets. The goal is to sell your stuff for more than it costs to manufacture or buy and then the business can keep or re-invest the profits. The question is, how tough, do you REALLY, need to be? And why aren't women seen as tough enough to do the job? We give birth, we keep families together, we raise children, I think we are really, really tough. We are certainly tough enough.

I sometimes don't know what to think about my own beautiful daughter going into a career that is comprised of 95% men and 5% women if we are generous with our math. My daughter started flying airplanes when she was 11. Her father took her to the Oshkosh Air Show in Oshkosh, WI when she was 8 and I bought her the first of her flying lessons for her 11th birthday. She had to bring a pillow to her flight lessons for the first 2 years because she was too short to reach the rudders. But - I also bought her ice-skating lessons, gymnastic lessons, tap and jazz dance lessons, piano lessons, voice lessons, and karate lessons. I certainly had no agenda around her being a commercial airline pilot. It seemed like a cool thing for her to learn and to do as a hobby and would also look good on her college resume. My daughter is very brave and adventurous and I always thought flying lessons would keep her motivated and excited because she was doing something with her free time that was so different from her peers.

My daughter is almost always the only girl in the room, and certainly the ONLY girl in the cockpit. I think like me, she likes it. I think like me, it makes her feel special and different and she has told me that she is very good at "hanging with the boys." She also has a close circle of girlfriends who are pilots. But I think that her circle of 5 friends consists of the majority of women pilots under the age of 40 living in area around the 2nd largest airport in the country. I sometimes fear for her future experiences in terms of being treated equally. However, she has always known that by going into this field, her flying classes would not be filled with girls. It is a given. Not that many girls fly airplanes. Sad, but it's just true.

And maybe that has been my challenge over time. I really never expected there to be ceilings to our progress as women in the workforce, glass or otherwise, I really never expected things to change SO SLOWLY, I just really never expected to experience what I have experienced when I set off on this very curious work journey over 30 years ago. I had inflated expectations at the very best and flat-out crazy ideas at the very worst.

And I worry that my own selfish enamoration with being the only girl is not really helping the cause. I NEED other women colleagues. We ALL need other women colleagues. I need other strong women in the room too. I need to get over needing to feel special by being "only." Those feelings are not helping the cause. I need to be confident of my own abilities and not get by on my "onlyness."

This is not easy. I am very proud of my daughter because she is working in her own career to promote women in aviation, to help more girls to see flying as a viable and exciting career option. She doesn't need to be the only girl to be the best – or to feel special or to be successful. She is just doing what she loves to do and what she can do really well. And that is a very true and good thing.

Business Wisdom Nugget #14: If you are the only girl in the room, don't stop there. We need to pull other women into the room with us. And we need to know that other women sitting next to us are not going to diminish our own value. We need to be confident. We need to be MORE than just the only one.

15

NOW WHAT?

I am spending a lot of my time these days talking to women who are declaring that they are "done". Done with all of the corporate crap which included trying to figure out how to be assertive but not too aggressive, how to appear competent but not too overbearing and how to stand up for their ideas and projects without being too pushy. DONE.

What is unfortunate about these decisions from my viewpoint is that these declarations are coming from some of the smartest businesswomen that I know. As a male CEO, even if you don't care about hiring a compassionate leader or a leader that truly can motivate a team or a leader who actually listens to other people – even if you don't care about any of those things in your senior executives because they seem too "soft", these business colleagues of mine can make your corporations real-life PROFITS! Even if numbers and profits are all the CEO cares about, he is leaving MONEY on the table when these women fall out of workforce. Or get kicked out. Or feel pushed out. It's a waste of good business resources and truly good business leaders do not waste resources. They leverage them. Hello? Mr. CEO? How can you actively ignore the disappearance of a resource that can make YOU money?

I am watching my 24-year-old daughter, who was born in 1991, and her friends, very carefully. It is far too early to tell how their careers will unfold. I see them just as optimistic, energetic, smart, capable and driven as my generation born in 1959. But, maybe there is a subtle different set of expectations from these young women. An expectation that they ARE needed. An expectation that their job is "just a job." An expectation that THEY are going to set the ground rules for how they are going to work for you. I don't see the fear in these young women that I felt and often saw in my generation of female colleagues. Rather than creating careers, it seems they are looking at an "exchange of services" type of relationship with their

52

current and future companies. These young women are saying, I will do "this" for you, Mr. Business Owner, and you will pay me. BUT, if you piss me off too much, I will go do "this" for someone else. Next. Why not? They are young and they can.

When my daughter was recently sick with a head cold, she stayed home from work for TWO WHOLE DAYS. I was shocked and also highly impressed. I almost always went to work even when I was almost dead. I went to work sick a whole lot of the time. I went to work on crutches; I went to work in pain. I would sleep in my car at lunch because I felt so horrible but I just didn't want to have to "call in sick." Missing two whole days of work was just unthinkable to me. Yet, my daughter did it and did NOT lose her job, and was able to get healthy staying at home and NOT infect her fellow colleagues and then go back to doing her job. She is loyal. She is skilled. But she was sick and she wasn't going to work sick. Sanity is such a great thing to watch. I pray that she can hold on to that thinking. Maybe I can catch it too!

For those of us women who grew up in the business world so very long ago, I see some very interesting and brave choices being made. Women who are starting their "own thing". Women who are starting their own thing and doing a part-time thing. Women doing 2 part-time things. Women doing project work and free-lance work. Women doing non-profit work and also non-paid volunteer work. Women making brave and fierce choices that honor who they are, their skills, their hearts and ultimately, their souls.

My current catchy business line is that "I am willing to date you but I don't want to get married." My heart belongs to me these days and probably always should have in retrospect. It's hard for me to imagine going back into a work environment where I "give my all" for a corporation. It sounds even kind of stupid to say that. My loyalty is to God and my family and wanting to use my gifts – those things that I am really good at doing. If you are a crazy CEO or CMO, I am simply NOT going to work for you. I don't care if you are the owner, that wonderful person who had the ONE great idea (and it is usually is, just ONE great idea that gets played out for the next 30 years), I am not going to babysit you and your ego. I don't care if you are famous in your own mind. If the work isn't a good fit for ME, I am not going to take it. I am being selective. I am looking at my "career" differently now.

I am in the process of changing my lifestyle. I no longer run out and buy the latest "It" bag. I buy my clothes at Target. Okay, I still buy some things at Nordstrom, but not much. And I find that I am OK with that. Some of the retail therapy I used to indulge in was just that – therapy to make me feel better because I was so frustrated with my work stressors and environment.

I absolutely love to mentor young women in business. I am perhaps a strange mentor choice only because I feel like I know so little about what ANYONE should do in their career journey. But after watching my daughter and deconstructing my own work path, I am leaning towards advising women to do something they really like. I have come full circle in my own thinking.

The business world has changed dramatically since 1981. The culture has changed dramatically since 1981. So… really…. can't we get a few more girls in the room to liven things up a bit? And maybe even, make you some money???

YES.

Business Wisdom Nugget #15: Okay, I surrender!! Do what you love and the money will follow! I think that could work… since I don't have a lot of experience doing that, I can't say for sure. But hey, it's worth a try, right? Onward!!!!! Let's Go!!!!!!

ABOUT THE AUTHOR

Nancy Louise Keyser Hamlin Bullock entered the corporate business world in 1981 and has been wondering why ever since. Her passion in her work life is writing and speaking and her passion in her personal life is focused on God, her husband and children. She writes and speaks about business issues and women in leadership and is President of *Digital Market Solutions, Inc.* She is still, very often, the only girl in the room.

51912565R00037